SandCastle 3

Long Vowels

Sometimes

Yȳ

Mary Elizabeth Salzmann

ABDO
Publishing Company

Published by SandCastle™, an imprint of ABDO Publishing Company, 4940 Viking Drive, Edina, Minnesota 55435.

Printed in the United States.

Cover and Interior Photo credits: Digital Vision, Eyewire Images, John Foxx Images, Photodisc, Rubberball Productions

Library of Congress Cataloging-in-Publication Data

Salzmann, Mary Elizabeth, 1968-
    Yy / Mary Elizabeth Salzmann.
      p. cm. -- (Long vowels)
    Includes index.
    ISBN 1-57765-418-8
      1. Readers (Primary) [1. English language--Phonetics.] I. Title.

PE1119 .S23426 2000
428.1--dc21

00-033210

The SandCastle concept, content, and reading method have been reviewed and approved by a national advisory board including literacy specialists, librarians, elementary school teachers, early childhood education professionals, and parents.

Let Us Know

After reading the book, SandCastle would like you to tell us your stories about reading. What is your favorite page? Was there something hard that you needed help with? Share the ups and downs of learning to read. We want to hear from you! To get posted on the Abdo Publishing Company Web site, send us email at:

sandcastle@abdopub.com

About SandCastle™
Nonfiction books for the beginning reader

- Basic concepts of phonics are incorporated with integrated language methods of reading instruction. Most words are short, and phrases, letter sounds, and word sounds are repeated.

- Readability is determined by the number of words in each sentence, the number of characters in each word, and word lists based on curriculum frameworks.

- Full-color photography reinforces word meanings and concepts.

- "Words I Can Read" list at the end of each book teaches basic elements of grammar, helps the reader recognize the words in the text, and builds vocabulary.

- Reading levels are indicated by the number of flags on the castle.

Look for more SandCastle books
in these three reading levels:

Level 1 (one flag)	**Level 2** (two flags)	**Level 3** (three flags)

Grades Pre-K to K 5 or fewer words per page	**Grades K to 1** 5 to 10 words per page	**Grades 1 to 2** 10 to 15 words per page

I know fun ways to make the time fly by.

What do you want to try?

Ely has a model plane.

It can fly high in the sky.

Ryan puts the recycling out by the street to be picked up.

Blythe is dyeing her
egg blue.

Then she will let it dry.

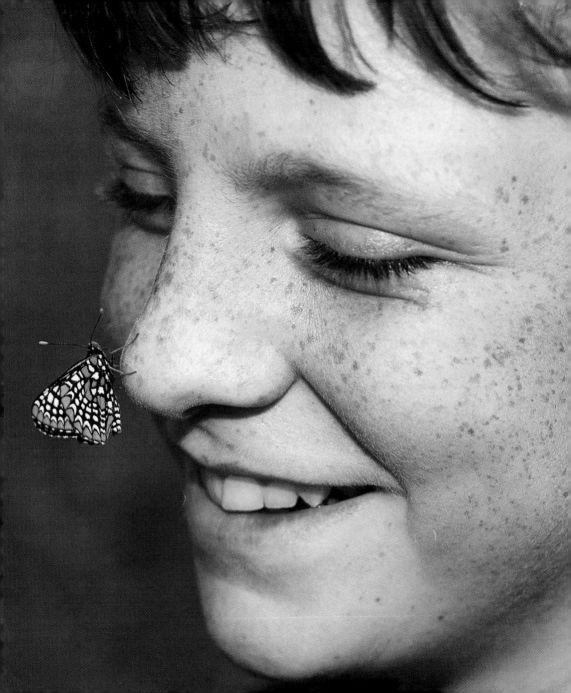

Lyle has a butterfly on his nose.

Soon it will fly away.

Kelly found a bunny in the mailbox.

What a funny place for a bunny!

Ruby and Yves are at a birthday party.

They eat cake and sing "Happy Birthday."

17

Yvette has strawberry juice on her face and shirt.

It is very sticky.

Yvonne has a cuddly friend.

What kind of animal is Yvonne holding?

(puppy)

Words I Can Read

Nouns

A noun is a person, place, or thing

animal (AN-uh-muhl)
  p. 21
bunny (BUHN-ee) p. 15
butterfly
  (BUHT-ur-flye) p. 13
cake (KAYK) p. 17
egg (EG) p. 11
face (FAYSS) p. 19
friend (FREND) p. 21

juice (JOOS) p. 19
kind (KINDE) p. 21
mailbox (MAYL-boks)
  p. 15
nose (NOHZ) p. 13
party (PAR-tee) p. 17
place (PLAYSS) p. 15
plane (PLANE) p. 7

puppy (PUHP-ee) p. 21
recycling (ree-SYE-
  kling) p. 9
shirt (SHURT) p. 19
sky (SKYE) p. 7
street (STREET) p. 9
time (TIME) p. 5
ways (WAYZ) p. 5

Proper Nouns

A proper noun is the name
of a person, place, or thing

Blythe (BLITHE) p. 11
Ely (EE-lye) p. 7
"Happy Birthday"
  (HAP-ee BURTH-
  day) p. 17

Kelly (KEL-ee) p. 15
Lyle (LILE) p. 13
Ruby (ROO-bee) p. 17
Ryan (RYE-uhn) p. 9

Yves (EEVZ) p. 17
Yvette (ee-VET) p. 19
Yvonne (ee-VON) p. 21

Pronouns

A pronoun is a word that replaces a noun

I (EYE) p. 5
it (IT) pp. 7, 11, 13, 19

she (SHEE) p. 11
they (THAY) p. 17

what (WUHT) pp. 5, 21
you (YOO) p. 5

22

Verbs

A verb is an action or being word

are (AR) p. 17
be (BEE) p. 9
can (KAN) p. 7
do (DOO) p. 5
dry (DRYE) p. 11
dyeing (DYE-ing) p. 11
eat (EET) p. 17
found (FOUND) p. 15

fly (FLYE) pp. 5, 7, 13
has (HAZ) pp. 7, 13, 19, 21
holding (HOHLD-ing) p. 21
is (IZ) pp. 11, 19, 21
know (NOH) p. 5
let (LET) p. 11

make (MAKE) p. 5
picked (PIKT) p. 9
puts (PUTSS) p. 9
sing (SING) p. 17
try (TRYE) p. 5
want (WONT) p. 5
will (WIL) pp. 11, 13

Adjectives

An adjective describes something

birthday (BURTH-day) p. 17
blue (BLOO) p. 11
cuddly (CUDH-uhl-ee) p. 21

fun (FUHN) p. 5
funny (FUH-nee) p. 15
her (HUR) pp. 11, 19
his (HIZ) p. 13

model (MOD-uhl) p. 7
sticky (STIK-ee) p. 19
strawberry (STRAW-ber-ee) p. 19
what (WUHT) p. 15

Adverbs

An adverb tells how, when, or where something happens

by (BYE) p. 5
away (uh-WAY) p. 13
high (HYE) p. 7

out (OUT) p. 9
soon (SOON) p. 13
then (THEN) p. 11

up (UHP) p. 9
very (VER-ee) p. 19

Glossary

animal – any living creature that can breathe and move about.

butterfly – a thin insect with large brightly colored wings.

mailbox – a container that letters and packages are delivered to.

recycling – items such as bottles and cans that can be used to make new products.

More Yȳ Words

any	fry	only
baby	hurry	pony
cry	July	shy
duty	lucky	type
early	my	why